Contribitors

Pastor Rick Dressler
Trent Kenney
Trevor Burton
Pastor Andrew McCombe
Jeff Mardling
Justin Egan
Jeremy Van Kesteren
Ethan Davenport
Pastor Dan Christiaans
S.J.M

I0528397

LIVING IN LIGHT OF THE **CROSS**
MAGAZINE

Editor in Chief: S. Jeyran Main
Publisher: Review Tales Publishing & Editing Services
Cover Design: Samantha Egan
Designs: Pexels
ISBN 978-1-988680-44-6 Paperback
ISBN 978-1-988680-43-9 Digital
www.MapleCityBaptistChurch.com
For all inquiries please contact us directly.

LIVING IN LIGHT OF THE CROSS MAGAZINE
MAPLE CITY BAPTIST CHURCH

Editor's Note

Dear Readers,

Welcome to the inaugural edition of "Living in Light of the Cross," a seasonal magazine by Maple City Baptist Church lovingly presented to you. As we embark on this spiritual journey together, we aim to enrich our faith and bring the Word of God into the everyday moments of our lives.

In each edition, we will delve into a book of the Bible, starting with the book of James for our spring issue. We hope that you will find inspiration, hope, and guidance through the testimonials and insightful articles shared by our diverse church family—comprising of members, pastors, and deacons.

This magazine is dedicated to deepening our relationship with Jesus Christ, offering peace, joy, and strength to navigate life's challenges. In a world that often seems divided, we embrace diversity and inclusivity, striving to be a heartfelt guide to living with kindness, compassion, and wisdom. It's about inspiring each of us to lead a life of selflessness in light of the cross.

I want to extend my deepest gratitude to everyone who contributed to making this first edition a reality. Your hard work, dedication, and faith have been instrumental in bringing this vision to life. As we distribute this magazine worldwide, we intend to spread the word of Jesus, offering hope and assurance that He is our everlasting Savior.

Thank you for joining us on this journey. May "Living in Light of the Cross" be a source of light and inspiration in our lives as we all strive to live more fully in His grace.

Blessings,

Jeyran Main

Editor-in-Chief
Living in Light of the Cross Magazine

MAPLE CITY BAPTIST CHURCH DOCUMENTARY

Introduction

Our home church, which fills our Sabbath-Sunday's with joyous morning worship and fellowship, engages our weeknights with activity and study programs for all ages earnestly seeks ways to serve and develop first our congregants and our community of Chatham-Kent. Like all churches, it has a remarkable history and origin story. We wish to bring honor in remembering how our wonderful church came to be.

There is so much here that God has taught us. A deeper level of faithful perseverance that, in our faithfulness to the Doctrine(s) of His Word alone, brings us to anticipate a beautiful future of service unto Him. We are a Baptist, membership-governed, church leadership-led church with the Word of God and Living Faith in Christ being of the utmost importance in the "culture" of our church.

Pastor Rick Dressler has shared with us in our membership classes an Acrostic on the fundamentals of being a Baptist believer in MCBC:

B - Biblical Authority (The Holy Bible is our authority!)

A - Autonomy of the local church (the local church has a responsibility to preach and teach in our community)

P - Priesthood of the believer (we who are saved are "priests" of the Lord, and Christ is our only Mediator)

T - Two Ordinances (Baptism and the Lord's Supper)

I - Individual Soul Liberty (all will give an account of themselves before God)

S - Saved and Baptised Church Membership (regenerated members of our church)

T- Two Offices of the Church (Elders and Deacons)

Origin

Maple City Baptist Church officially began in 1978. While there is much to be said about our Evangelical Baptist denomination that we stand by (that is- the Baptist denominational strand that originated from a sect of the Church of England by John Smith [who became a separatist that merged the reformed Baptist faith into Holland], and accredited to have been brought over and implemented in North America by the missionary, Roger Williams), we as a local church began at that time as a house-gathered church in a home close to our current church location.

This small group of believers gathered in the home church enjoyed their time studying and communion with our Lord God and eventually were led to pursue expansion by purchasing a local church property. In 1979, a congregant of the church by the name of Dick Person made the purchase deal with a local farmer who owned the land at the time that is now the place of our current church property. When the deal had solidified and closed, the church building was being built together by the hands of the congregants. With a Second Temple of Nehemiah-like zeal, they worked together and began crafting our church building.

Perseverance In Our Trials

Pastor Rick Dressler began his position here at MCBC in the Lord's Ministry in 2001. The church has had trials since, including the COVID-19 pandemic.

When navigating through this after the initial lockdown(s), the pastoral and elder team and devoted congregants purchased cameras, an FM transmitter, and other accommodations for supporting services. Numerous Sunday services were offered at the time to accommodate those brought to worship in person under lockdown group size restrictions and offer online streaming.

Through our trials, the congregation grew numerically and spiritually.

Our Vision Furthermore

First and foremost, Maple City Baptist Church is for the Good News of our Lord Jesus Christ!

We are blessed to see what God is doing here in the lives of our congregation, our Sunday Morning Services, our weekly programs that offer a family community and minister to all different "walks of life," our active service in blessing our local community of Chatham-Kent, etc.

Trials that were faced that seemed to be a taxing uphill climb have proved to be times of growth where the Lord showed us that persevering in faith and keeping our hearts and minds centered on Him often brings the fruit(s) of blessing. This growth principle is something that we can implement further in our local community.

MCBC welcomes you with open arms, and we wish you an encounter of Christ's Grace in your life.

Trent Kenney, along with his wife, Samantha, and son, Ezra, joined Maple City Baptist Church in November 2023, having moved from Huntsville, ON. With a background in Creative Writing from Fleming College and a graduate of Heritage College & Seminary, Trent's passion for writing, especially faith-based articles, ignited during his tenure as Youth & Children's Ministries Director/Pastor at Minden Bible Church. His experience in ministry fueled his love for teaching and later transitioned into writing for platforms like Medium and Koinonia Publication, with work published in LOVE IS MOVING magazine. His diverse career includes roles as Warehouse Manager for Mark's, residential carpenter in Muskoka, Service Advisor for Hyundai Canada, and grocery clerk, among others. Currently, Trent works in the Service department for Hyundai of Chatham, continuing his career with Hyundai Canada.

Trevor Burton, a lifelong Chatham-Kent resident, found salvation at 39 during the Covid pandemic, joining Maple City Baptist Church in June 2020 as it grew amidst global uncertainty. Raised in Ridgetown with a deep interest in the arts, he pursued film studies at the Toronto Film School, graduating with high honors in 2006, initially aspiring to create horror and culturally relevant films without a focus on spiritual themes. Facing personal challenges, including depression, alcoholism, and loss, in his late 20s and 30s, he turned to faith through the influence of a close friend and church member, leading to a transformative acceptance of Jesus Christ. Shifting away from his former film ambitions, Trevor now focuses on projects honoring his faith, works as a warehouse clerk and key holder, and cherishes time with his church and children.

COUNT IT ALL JOY

PASTOR DRESSLER

James opens his letter to a group of people facing difficult times. Dispersed across the Roman Empire, many have lost family, friends, and their livelihoods, with some even undergoing tremendous persecution. Amidst these challenges, James instructs them in verse 2 to "count it all joy when you fall into various trials." The term "count" serves as an imperative command in Greek, suggesting to "hold the view or opinion." Thus, James advises this beleaguered group of believers to adopt a stance of joy amidst their trials —an idea that may seem counterintuitive.

What does it mean "to hold the opinion" of joy? James isn't suggesting we feign happiness or force a smile. Nor is he implying that joy naturally accompanies trials. Instead, the joy referenced here aligns with the concept of grace—a gift, a treasure, something to be cherished, intrinsically linked to God. It is a deliberate choice to perceive trials through the lens of joy, recognizing them as a grace, treasure, and gift from God.

The term "trial" refers to the process of discovering the character or nature of someone or something through extensive testing, aiming to reveal the true essence of a person or thing, not merely what we believe or pretend to be.

James encourages us to consciously decide to embrace joy as tests and trials unveil our true selves. In a fallen world, fulfilling this command may appear daunting, if not unattainable. How can we adhere to this directive? James provides guidance, explaining that understanding the purpose and outcome of trials in our lives is crucial. Without this insight, we might feel perplexed, frustrated, or even bitter.

Life is full of challenges—broken cars, strained relationships, grief, pain, and loss. Yet, James reassures us that God doesn't let our experiences go to waste. These trials foster patience, enabling us to endure and remain steadfast, strengthening our moral character. He further explains in verse 4, "Let patience have her perfect work," emphasizing that trials are meant to mature and mold us into the image of His Son.

Joni Eareckson Tada's story exemplifies this teaching. At 17, a diving accident left her quadriplegic, leading to depression and suicidal thoughts. Her plea to God, "If I can't die, show me how to live," was answered with a life of profound joy. Now, at over 74, her ministry is a testament to finding joy in trials and growing into the image of Jesus.

In sum, James's message to count it all joy amidst trials is a powerful reminder of the transformative power of embracing trials with a godly perspective, knowing that God uses these experiences for our growth and His glory.

Pastor Dressler

In July 2001, Pastor Dressler was called to move his family to Chatham to pastor a church struggling with only 23 people. He, his wife, Kim, and their three sons trusted the Lord and made Canada their new home. They would later add a fourth son, Andy! His plan was simple: preach the Word of God and exalt the Lord Jesus Christ. It has been amazing to watch the Lord bless His work here! Christ has been exalted, and men and women are being drawn to Him. A loving Church and a family atmosphere have blessed us! Our family has grown, too! We have four daughters-in-law and nine grandchildren! We invite you to come and see what God is doing here at Maple City Baptist Church.

DOERS OF THE WORD

PASTOR ANDREW MCCOMBE

James 1:22-25 (NKJV) states, "But be doers of the word, and not hearers only, deceiving yourselves. For if anyone is a hearer of the word and not a doer, he is like a man observing his natural face in a mirror, for he observes himself, goes away, and immediately forgets what kind of man he was. But he who looks into the perfect law of liberty and continues in it, and is not a forgetful hearer but a doer of the work, this one will be blessed in what he does."

In 2 Timothy 3:16-17, the apostle Paul reminds his student, Timothy, that all Scripture is God-breathed and is profitable for doctrine, for reproof, for correction, for instruction in righteousness, so that the man of God may be complete, thoroughly equipped for every good work. This passage highlights two principles: first, God's Word is inerrant, meaning it is without error, and second, God's Word is sufficient for every aspect of the Christian life to sanctify God's people and conform them to the image of Christ.

James 1:22-25 echoes these truths, urging readers to hear the Word and be doers of the Word. This presents a significant challenge among Canadian Christians in the twenty-first century. While many are willing to affirm the inerrancy of God's Word, there is often a failure to act upon it or to submit to its sufficiency in our lives. Recognizing God's Word as sufficient for every aspect of our Christian lives is crucial; otherwise, we remain mere hearers.

Emulating Christ's humility is essential for obedience. Philippians 2:5-8 demonstrates Christ's humility and servitude, highlighting that He was not only a hearer but a doer of

God's will, even unto death on the cross. To acknowledge the sufficiency of God's Word, we must follow Jesus Christ's example and humble ourselves by being doers of the Word.

The gospel compels true followers of Christ to act upon the Word, not out of legalistic obligation but inspired by the Holy Spirit dwelling within us. This enables us to joyfully obey the Word, even in times of difficulty and persecution, as described in James 1:3. Reflecting on Christ's obedience, as narrated in John 17, before His arrest, is a powerful reminder of our call to obedience.

James 1:25 reveals the loving-kindness of our heavenly Father, who provides His Word for guidance and empowers us through His Spirit to be doers of the Word. He promises blessings for those who demonstrate their faith through action. What a magnificent God we serve! Let us humbly adhere to the teachings of 2 Timothy 3:16-17 and James 1:22-25, living each day in the light of Christ's sacrifice, striving not just to be hearers but doers of the Word.

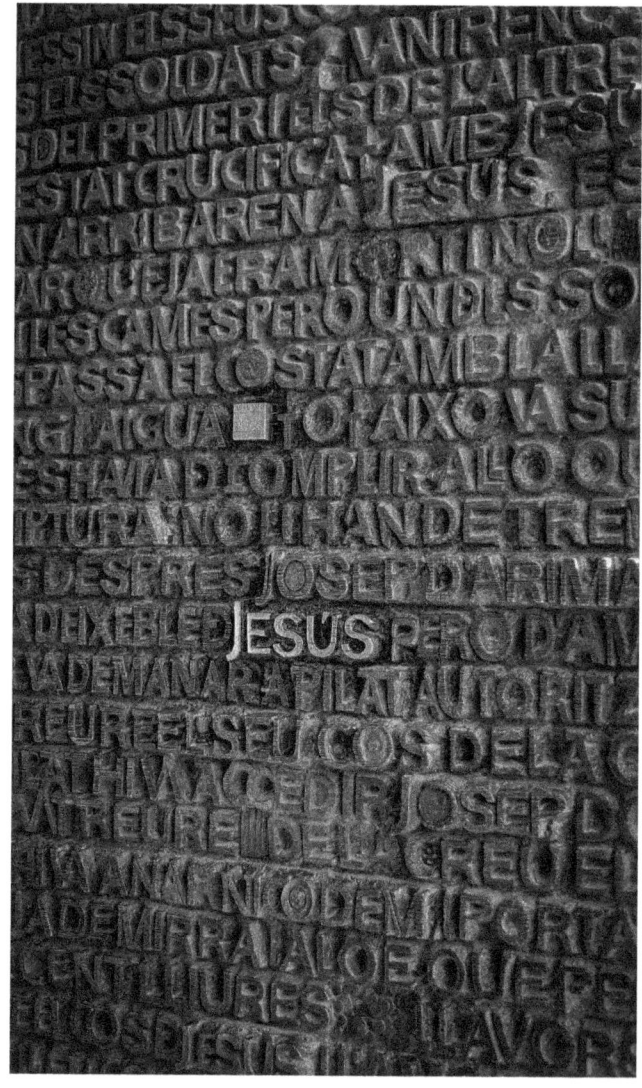

Pastor Andrew McCombe

Andrew McCombe grew up in London, Ontario. He attended Liberty University, where he received his teaching degree and met his wife, Stacey, who also grew up in London. Surprisingly, their paths didn't cross until school in Virginia.

Andrew enjoyed teaching at Chatham Christian School for eight years, where his burden for the students and church grew. God developed a strong yearning within him to serve in full-time ministry at MCBC. As the church grew, so did the need for additional pastoral leadership. He is pursuing his Master of Divinity and is thankful for the opportunity to learn under MCBC's faithful pastors.

He has spent the last eight years serving here in various ministries. He has a special burden to encourage families to take a stand for truth, even amid uncomfortable times. He sees the value of growing a strong foundation and preaches and teaches the Word with conviction. He and his wife, Stacey, have four children. They have loved serving alongside the saints at MCBC and hope to do so for as long as God allows.

GOD GRANTS GRACE TO THE HUMBLE
JEFF MARDLING

Dear friends, have you shared your faith today, in the last week, month, or year? We are living in tumultuous times. Our culture is steeped in sin, and there is a desperate need for the power of the gospel to spread throughout the world and for lost souls to be spiritually reborn and saved. Perhaps you find yourself struggling in your daily walk with the Lord Jesus Christ. You recognize the urgency to reach the lost but wrestle with life's routines and pressures, especially when considering the call to walk humbly and righteously with the Lord.

James chapter 4, verses 1-10, serves as a bright light and a wake-up call for both believers and sinners. It issues a stern warning to Christians to remember that God dwells within you and that the call to holiness is paramount in your sanctification. Consider how seriously you dedicate yourself to God's teachings compared to the allurements of this world. Are you not aware that friendship with the world is enmity with God? (v. 4)

Reflecting on nearly 22 years of walking with Jesus, it became clear early on that the Holy Spirit would lead me to regularly share my faith and equip other Christians to do the same.

My journey included witnessing to family, friends, and acquaintances, joining a team of believers burdened to witness the gospel from the church, distributing gospel tracts, engaging in one-on-one conversations, and eventually being called to preach openly in the streets. I often turned to this passage as the basis for calling men and women to repentance and faith in Christ. It became a foundation for explaining God's holiness and humanity's sinfulness and a springboard to share the love, mercy, and grace demonstrated at the cross.

"Do you not know that friendship with the world is enmity with God?" (v. 4) This verse excited me. It serves as a perfect way to urge lost sinners to stop living for themselves and the world and to repent and believe in the gospel.

A wise brother advised me to read the Bible with a 20/20 vision—examining the 20 verses before and after any focused text to understand God's message in context. This beautiful passage illuminates the truth in a man's soul and provides a fresh realization of James's message to the church. It is a divine charge to God's children to battle against the flesh and the world. It serves as a profound reminder and warning to avoid yielding to past passions and the desires of your heart and to be distinct from your neighbors.

Loved ones, if you find yourself in a season of dull faith or yearning to grow spiritually, consider how you spend your time. Embrace each day as a fresh start, always beginning with prayer and daily scripture reading. You will find sustenance and guidance to resist the devil, and the world's challenges will seem less burdensome. You will discover that wisdom from above is pure, peaceable, gentle, open to reason, full of mercy and good fruits, impartial, and sincere. A harvest of righteousness is sown in peace by those who make peace (3:17-18). Embrace these practices in light of the glorious gospel, and your heart will be equipped to live rightly with God, navigate this world, and share and spread His message of salvation with everyone you meet.

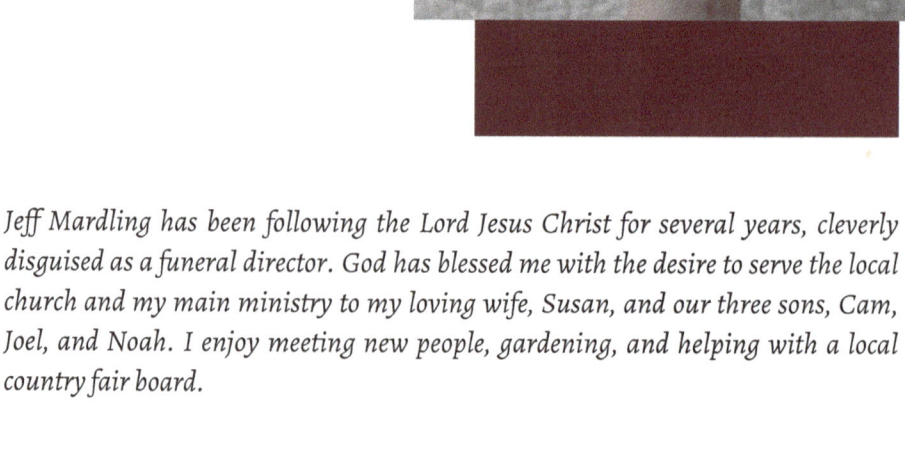

Jeff Mardling has been following the Lord Jesus Christ for several years, cleverly disguised as a funeral director. God has blessed me with the desire to serve the local church and my main ministry to my loving wife, Susan, and our three sons, Cam, Joel, and Noah. I enjoy meeting new people, gardening, and helping with a local country fair board.

Good and Perfect Gifts
Justin Egan

"Every good and perfect gift is from above, coming down from the Father of the heavenly lights, who does not change like shifting shadows."

The words of James 1:17 echoed in my ears as I peacefully floated in my canoe beneath thousands of stars and a moon bright enough to cast shadows on the liquid glass beneath me. It was my second trip to Algonquin Park and we were studying the book of James. Having canoed seemingly against the wind for several days and portaged through mud and mosquito-infested swamp, I had to keep reminding my aching and bug bit body that I am supposed to consider it joy when I face trials.

However, despite my aching shoulders and soggy shoes, the beauty and tranquility that surrounded me that evening in the middle of a serene lake was surreal. It was the first time that I thought about every good and perfect gift being from God. While this thought seemed explicitly elementary, it was the ruminating on it that created a new perspective for me. I already knew that 'perfect' meant complete.

Where I sat in still darkness, the sounds of distant loons echoing across the water, and the silhouettes of towering

pines against a backdrop of endless constellations seemed as close to perfection in that moment as I could be. However, realizing that the surrounding beauty was directly from God created a new sense of awe for me. In my finite mind, there was always the assumption that the "perfect gift" was that which fulfilled the recipient's desires. However, I had never considered that this "good and perfect gift" was that which completely accomplished what the giver intended in addition to benefiting the recipient.

What currently encompassed me was just a glimpse of God's beauty and power, a gift

intended to create awe and worship of our Savior and Creator. One might question how awe and worship of the gift giver might benefit the recipient. However, when we realize that God designed us to operate in a manner that starts with worshipping Him, only then can we experience true freedom from the bonds of our carnal nature. Jeremiah reminded us that the heart is deceitful above all things and beyond cure.

As I drifted among the placid aura, I meditated on the last half of the verse. The ambiance into which I had immersed myself made the words "Father of the heavenly lights" come alive.

The shifting outline of our Milky Way galaxy framed by innumerable stars shouted the grandeur of our God. Described as the "Father," they invoked characteristics of leader, protector, sustainer, and creator. That is what our Lord is to the glory of His creation.

He is the Creator and Sustainer of the lights literally on display in front of me. I watched the shadows dance on the water's surface as the brilliant moon reflected off rocks, logs, and trees. Unlike the dancing shadows that changed with each ripple and breeze, God's presence and characteristics remain consistent, a promise that brings with it peace and surety.

Justin Egan is a follower of Jesus Christ, a husband to an amazing wife, a father to five beautiful children, and an employee at an energy company. God keeps teaching him how important that order is even despite the many times that he keeps messing it up. He believes that it is through focus on Christ, effective collaboration, and leadership that success can be achieved and impacting change can occur. Justin holds degrees in electrical engineering and mathematics. Justin enjoys spending time with his wife and five kids, coaching soccer, spending time outdoors, and volunteering in his community.

Liberation In Christlike Humility When Facing A Busy Life

HOW WE MAY PURSUEHUMILITY, FOCUS ON OUR ETERNALREWARD(S), AND ADORATION OF CHRIST IN OUR OCCUPATIONS

TRENT KENNEY

We have all experienced that transitional time in our lives in adolescence when we start to obtain our responsibilities, begin to pursue our desires in life, and anticipate a supposed "freedom" when we go out on our own and "spread our wings," etc.

Do you remember in your own life what this was like when you reached adulthood and had a pocket full of dreams when going off on your life and establishing your individualism?

Now, let's fast-forward to the stage you are at now in your life.

That original novelty now seems like a sort of "past life experience," so to speak.

While it may be difficult to pinpoint when exactly that excitement seems to wilt and wither away, we may now be at a point where life can feel like a bewildering mix of monotony and overwhelm. At times, it may seem as if our labor and general life efforts are in vain.

Humble yourselves before the LORD, and he will lift you up. NIV

James 4:10

There is a timeless example of someone who was attempting to do life without the Lord at the center and without first pursuing hope in Him (from a king, nonetheless!):

2 "Meaningless! Meaningless!" says the Teacher.

"Utterly meaningless! Everything is meaningless."

3 What do people gain from all their labors at which they toil under the sun?" (Ecclesiastes 1:2-3, NIV)

"10 Whoever loves money never has enough;

whoever loves wealth is never satisfied with their income. This, too, is meaningless.

11 As goods increase, so do those who consume them.

And what benefit are they to the owners except to feast their eyes on them?" (Ecclesiastes 5:10-11, NIV)

When we evaluate ourselves honestly, we may realize that our labors and possessions of this life are not everlasting. They will one day dwindle, and we will not take with us to eternity any possessions of this world.

However, our Lord Jesus has given us hope in Him that if, in our honest evaluation of ourselves, we seek specific ways in our individual lives, we may humble the pride of life and come to identity and dependence on Him in our day-to-day life pursuits that we may be investing in the eternal Kingdom of Heaven (Matthew 6:19-24).

Work schedules, chores for your home, and extracurricular commitments may, over time, become something we view on the calendar with a sigh and feelings of overwhelm. Time to budget finances with our spouse or for ourselves (depending on your situation) is postponed to later times that keep getting pushed back. Personal care time, fulfilling the "love tank" of a spouse, investing time and attention into a community, and participating in family traditions consequently become a means to additional burnout. And oh! By the way! We should put our communal time with our Lord Jesus first on the priority list and spend time in His presence, praying and meditating on His Holy Word!

Is it possible that we idolize this life's occupations rather than rightfully worshiping the Lord who created it?

Are we becoming proud of our lives, wearing our busyness as a badge of social status?

A passage from James makes me ponder these points and brings me to realize the fragility of life and that only our Lord and our Saving Grace in Him ought to be what we use our life occupations to serve for, in turn investing in our eternity:

13 Now listen, you who say, "Today or tomorrow, we will go to this or that city, spend a year there, carry on business, and make money." 14 Why, you do not even know what will happen tomorrow. What is your life? You are a mist that appears for a little while and then vanishes. 15 Instead, you should say, "If it is the Lord'swill, we will live and do this or that." (James 4:13-15, NIV)

Let us not become numb to adoring our Lord, but work and serve each day as an adoration unto Him.

Trent Kenney, *along with his wife, Samantha, and son, Ezra, joined Maple City Baptist Church in November 2023, having moved from Huntsville, ON. With a background in Creative Writing from Fleming College and a graduate of Heritage College & Seminary, Trent's passion for writing, especially faith-based articles, ignited during his tenure as Youth & Children's Ministries Director/Pastor at Minden Bible Church. His experience in ministry fueled his love for teaching and later transitioned into writing for platforms like Medium and Koinonia Publication, with work published in LOVE IS MOVING magazine. His diverse career includes roles as Warehouse Manager for Mark's, residential carpenter in Muskoka, Service Advisor for Hyundai Canada, and grocery clerk, among others. Currently, Trent works in the Service department for Hyundai of Chatham, continuing his career with Hyundai Canada.*

JAMES *the Brother of Our Lord*

Jeremy Van Kesteren

In the introduction to the first edition of his German New Testament in 1522, Martin Luther famously remarked, "Therefore, Saint James's epistle is a right strawy epistle in comparison with them (Romans, Galatians, Ephesians, and 1 Peter), for it has no gospel character to it." Although Luther never denied the inspiration of James, such a statement from a theologian of his stature could discourage laypeople from engaging in healthy debate about the text. Consequently, this rich book often doesn't receive the attention and study it rightly deserves, in my opinion.

Attempting to write something inventive about this book feels too daunting for me. Instead, I approach the Bible by trying to understand the context, both historical and grammatical, and then reflect on how it aligns with what God has taught me in my life.

In his greeting to the twelve tribes, James introduces himself not as the brother of our Lord, as one might expect, but as a servant of God. The Greek word used, "Doulos," translates to "slave," but it signifies not an unwilling slave, but a committed, willing servant.

Growing up with Jesus, James and his siblings were initially unconvinced of His Lordship and mission on Earth.

The wisdom they were exposed to through Jesus' words and actions must have been extraordinary. It's plausible that the content and structure of his epistle, mirroring Matthew 5 and 7, offer insights into what he learned from his older brother. However, it wasn't until after Jesus' crucifixion and resurrection that they truly believed. From that moment, James transformed from a skeptical sibling to a fearless leader, urging his followers to live lives worthy of their calling, a conviction that ultimately led to his martyrdom in 62 AD.

Overlooking James due to its supposed lack of teaching on the core doctrines of Christianity is misguided. The emphasis on holy living, testing of faith, and righteous works in response to salvation offers incredibly practical advice for Christians.

James, more than anyone, understood the contrast between the truth he eventually embraced and the falsehoods of his upbringing, falsehoods perpetuated by the Pharisees and Sadducees, whom Jesus vehemently criticized.

The book of James underscores the importance of unwavering obedience to God's Word. Each time I study James, whether through my men's group or our pastor's sermons, it speaks to me anew, challenging me to

Jeremy Van Kesteren, married to Joeline, father of ten blessings, grandfather, child of the most high.

find joy in trials or to guard my speech. While it's difficult to choose a favorite verse from James, one particularly resonant passage is: "Count it all joy, my brothers, when you meet trials of various kinds, for you know that the testing of your faith produces steadfastness. And let steadfastness have its full effect, that you may be perfect and complete, lacking in nothing." James 1:2-4. This verse encapsulates the enduring and transformative message of James, inviting us to embrace trials as opportunities for growth and completeness in faith.

Reflections on Redemption

Ethan Davenport

My life has been one of nothing but grace. On March 28th, 2021, I attended Maple City Baptist Church for the first time, knowing nothing of Christianity. I came from a secular home with two very loving parents, a younger brother, and the two most adorable dogs in all creation. Growing up in an upper-middle-class home, I enjoyed many material pleasures and familial joys. However, the greatest happiness was absent from my life.

On that last Sunday of March 2021, the congregation sang triumphantly, "O sing hallelujah! / Our hope springs eternal," [1] I felt goosebumps.

Ethan Davenport is 18 years old. He began attending Maple City in 2021 and was baptized in 2022. He is currently completing his Bachelor of Arts at Hillsdale College in Hillsdale, Michigan.

Hearing that old English proverb sung aloud, I knew it to be true—hope is eternal in the human heart. But what does man have to hope for? It was a sweet revelation when God answered this question for me.

Over the next few months, I regularly attended Maple City, eventually visiting a boys' youth gathering. Although spiritually dead and reluctant to surrender to the true Christ, I was curious about the Christian faith. My first experience with Pastor Dan evolved from a Bible lesson into a Q&A session on biology and the Christian religion. Week after week, the Lord drew me back to His people, and the truths Pastor Rick's preaching began to resonate with me.

Even as a proud sixteen-year-old, I knew I was not God. With time, I realized the condition of my soul was not desirable. Despite having heard the gospel many times, I had never truly listened. I was content with God being an idea, an object of contemplation, or a moral imperative for societal improvement. I had stripped God of His nature and was comfortable doing so.

Then, I was born again. In one moment, I was a spiritual corpse in bondage to sin; in the next, I was a child of the King. I lived Titus 3:3-7. Ethan Davenport had received a heart transplant. The Holy Spirit resurrected me, and I was alive—and now I loved Jesus Christ. Though not perfect, I was seen as such in God's eyes. My knees were wobbly, and my legs were frail, but I now stood on solid ground. I no longer sought fulfillment in lesser things but in the greatest fulfillment, which is God. I no longer wished to grieve the One who died for me. For the first time, I had tasted and seen the sweetness of our Triune God. My soul had feasted on all He is for us in Christ; the eternal hope I sang of on my first Lord's Day had finally found its object. My soul was completely satisfied.

As I write this piece, I can't help but grin, considering once again the overwhelming joy of my salvation. Knowing I have nothing to offer Him, God chose to give Himself to me. Christian, this is true for you, too. The God who could justly strike us dead for our rebellion and separate Himself from us chose instead to take on human flesh, live a life of obedience we never could, and bear our eternal punishment on that miserable cross. He wore red stripes so we could wear white robes. We have nothing to offer Jesus, but He offers Himself to us. His greatest gift is not merely eternal life or freedom from sin; His greatest gift to us is Himself. Delight in Him! Immerse yourself in the Bible, pray, and enjoy sweet communion with His saints. Lastly, run to our Lord with every want and need, for "God is most glorified in us when we are most satisfied in Him." [2]

[1] "Christ Our Hope in Life and Death," by Keith and Kristyn Getty.
[2] John Piper's summary of the philosophy of the Christian life.

Pastor Dan Christiaans has served at Maple City Baptist Church as a Youth and Associate Pastor for 19 years. He and his wife, Tara, have eight children.

Hope in the

DOMINIC REPUBLIC

Pastor Dan Christiaans

Introduction

One of the great joys of pastoring is witnessing what God is doing worldwide. In December of 2023, a small team from Maple City was privileged to visit the ministries we support in the Dominican Republic under the leadership of Pastor Yves Talleyrand. There, nestled down busy, narrow roads in the heart of an underprivileged Haitian neighborhood, you will find Christ the Redeemer Baptist Church, a ministry I have grown to love and one I want you to know more about. This article will chronicle the story of Yves and his wife, Naomie, and explain how God led our church to support them.

Ministry Beginnings

Yves grew up in Haiti and participated in the Compassion International child sponsorship program. He credits the support he received from his sponsors with the privilege of attending elementary school, graduating high school, and attending undergraduate classes in theology, law, and medicine. By God's grace, Yves has worked hard to better himself; he now speaks five languages and is a talented singer and musician. His heart has always been to serve the Lord; he began training for ministry in a Baptist church in Haiti. Around this time, Yves married a wonderful woman named Naomie, moved to the Dominican Republic, and had a son named Yvesno. Yves planted his first church in Haiti and realized the Lord had gifted him to do this. Since then, he has planted many more churches in the DR and Haiti, many of which still look to him for leadership.

From the Dominican Republic to Chatham, Ontario

Our elders were first introduced to Pastor Yves in 2015 when God providentially placed him in our office. At that time, we had only heard of Yves through an acquaintance and had no plan of supporting the ministry in the Dominican Republic; however, after sitting with Yves and hearing of God's work, the elders felt compelled to help.

That meeting occurred nine years ago; since then, Maple City has primarily supported Yves' ministry, FESSIF (you can learn more about his ministry at fessif.org). On top of regular support to the church ministry, we started a student sponsorship program that allows local, impoverished Haitian children to attend the Christian school. Yves' wife Naomie is the principal there, and the school employs many faithful teachers who work with students from junior kindergarten through grade eight. Two years ago, we were able to help them purchase property and a church building for the first time in Santiago de los Caballeros. We hope this location will provide a permanent site for gospel ministry for many years to come.

The Character of a Servant

I have had the privilege of building friendships with Yves over the past nine years. He lives a very modest lifestyle, but on many occasions, I've watched him make sacrifices to help those whom he deems to be in greater need than himself. If you give a gift to Yves, you must tell him he's not allowed to give it away; otherwise, he will! Everything he does is in response to two things. First, Jesus sent people to help him as a child when he was in desperate physical need. Most Haitian children are born with little hope; however, believers serving at Compassion International provided Yves with sustenance, healthcare, and education. The second and primary reason that Yves is so generous is the gospel. Jesus came for him when he was spiritually lost and hopeless. His life now belongs to Jesus because Jesus died to give him new life. He lives to bring the gospel of hope that he received to those with no hope. He works hard to pastor the church God has placed him in. He also wants to see other pastors equipped to serve the Lord; he helps guide men already pastoring those training to be pastors in the future. When you are in a room with Yves and his people, their respect and love for him is evident.

From Chatham to the Dominican Republic

This trip marks the fourth time I've visited his ministry; I was thrilled to bring my daughter, Avery, sister, Samantha, and friend, Isaak, with me. We met all the children at the school, played games with them at recess, and painted their classrooms. The church organized a family conference,

and I was grateful to speak with them about marriage and parenting from a biblical perspective. We enjoyed delicious Haitian cuisine prepared by Naomie and were included in morning and evening devotions. Celebrating the Lord's supper with their church family and dedicating three babies to Jesus were highlights for me. Yves also took us three hours southeast to visit a ministry that serves villages in the heart of the sugar cane fields called the "bateyes." It was amazing to see the impact these servants of Jesus have in such remote and isolated places. Worshipping Jesus with them was an honor; that experience has helped me gain greater anticipation for the day when every tongue, tribe, and nation will sing the praises of our Saviour and King.

Final Reflection

There are some things that you must see to understand. It isn't easy to describe what life is like for so many Haitians who are living in the Dominican Republic. They face poverty, racism, and hopelessness daily. It was a joy to have people I love with me, to watch as they fell in love with the people there, and to see them understand what life is like for those who happen to be born in a different place. The daily challenges are difficult to witness, but God is at work there, which is glorious; faithful servants around the country are spreading the hope of the gospel. We had the opportunity to see and be a small part of that work for a week, and I came home with a deepened desire to be a blessing to the ministry there. You can help, too! Funds donated to this ministry will go directly to the church and the school. I thank God for what He does through Yves, Naomie, and all those who serve with them. Please join me in praying for them as they serve.

LIVING AN AUTHENTIC CHRISTIAN LIFE

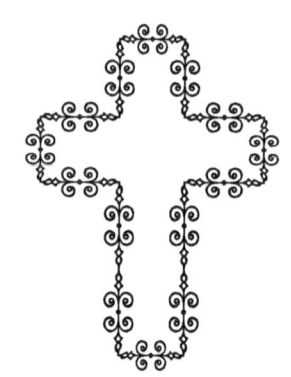

BY A CHURCH MEMBER

Are you satisfied with your life spiritually? If you're a Christian, you have faith in Jesus, know that he died for your sins, and try to live your life as a good person. But is that it? Is that what this is all about?

Let me tell you a bit about my story. I grew up in the church, was baptized as an infant, did a profession of faith at the age of 15, and about 12 years ago was baptized as an adult. My education was at Christian institutions; my extended family was Christian, and my friends were also Christian. I have read through my Bible several times, studied apologetics and theology, memorized pieces of the Heidelberg Catechism and Scripture, and attended church every Sunday (even twice a Sunday) unless I was sick. I have never questioned God; my faith has not wavered, and I know I am saved. But is that it? Do I just keep going along ticking these boxes in a mundane spiritual life?

To give you a better picture, I grew up in a church where faith was private and not discussed. A committee oversaw the process of bringing people to the church.

It was not on us as individuals to do that. Babies were baptized as soon as possible in case they died in infancy to ensure they would go to heaven. Profession of Faith was seen almost as a graduation from catechism classes, with pressure from parents to finish it. Life Monday to Saturday was lived how you wanted as long as you were in church Sunday morning, you prayed before and after every meal, read your Bible, and you were a good person.

In 2020, God started working in my life in a way that left me unsatisfied with how I lived. During COVID, I started watching church online and was repeatedly confronted with the truths of Scripture. After each sermon, I was left speechless with what was pulled out of the preached passages. This God I was hearing about wanted more from me, more from my life; he wasn't satisfied with me coasting along. That journey continued as I started attending Maple City Baptist Church. Again, week after week, I was convicted and motivated to change how I lived and viewed things. Let me reiterate: I have been a Christian for years.

Then I started reading the book "Gentle and Lowly" and realized I mistakenly put God in a box. Some of the things I learned from confident spiritual leaders and certain family members in previous churches were untrue. It was mixed with their traditions, people's warped views because of their experiences, or even people who were church leaders but were not actually spiritual leaders. It turns out that God the Father is not the harsh taskmaster in the Old Testament or that Jesus the Son was forced to take matters into his own hands and die on the cross because we bring too much shame (and we are still not good enough), or that the Holy Spirit is this other part of the trinity that we just don't talk about because we lack understanding. I have also viewed God as being too busy with the world's big issues to bother with me, and if I just keep my head down and my nose clean, I'll stay under the radar, and it'll all be good.

I was so wrong in my thinking, and I am so sorry to God for believing this. The truth is that Jesus' life shows his heart, the heart of the Father, and the Holy Spirit. God is there with open arms, wanting us to come to him. He can handle all of us going to him at the same time. He has time for us, patience for us, and overwhelming love for us. We confess our sins to him not for us to be shamed but for him to heal us. Did you know it gives him joy when we come to him, and when we choose not to, we deny him that joy?

I am so excited to be in this time of understanding more who this God of the universe actually is, and I am hungering to know him more fully each day. I am re-reading "Gentle and Lowly" and proving it with Scripture, letting it soak my heart and soul and change me. If you're reading this, I encourage you to self-reflect. Yes, you may be a Christian, but how are you different from the world? What does God really mean to you? How has your past molded your thinking, and is it true? If you don't have the book "Gentle and Lowly" I encourage you to get a copy and read it. Then, go back to the Bible to see how it lines up. I hope it will change your life and perspective forever, leaving you hungering to know him more fully each day.

I am thankful and excited to see how God continues to lead and use me for his purposes each day. I pray that we can all experience this God and the truth of who he is. I challenge you to get to know him and grow deeper each day. Don't be satisfied with the ticked boxes and living your life as it is.

JAMES 1:17

EVERY GOOD AND PERFECT GIFT IS FROM ABOVE, COMING DOWN FROM THE FATHER OF THE HEAVENLY LIGHTS, WHO DOES NOT CHANGE LIKE SHIFTING SHADOWS. NIV

JESUS WAS CALLING FOR ME

BY S.J.M

I had a dream. I dreamt that I was at a gathering, and there was a well-dressed man sitting on a chair at the head of the crowd. The moment I got there, the crowd divided, and I saw a path open between the person sitting on the chair and me. He appeared holy and handsome, and I knew he must be important. The holy man on the chair smiled at me and made a notion with his hands, asking me to go to him, so I moved forward. As I looked at the crowd, I saw men and women with normal human faces, but when I got to the holy man and stood next to him, I turned around. Suddenly, all their faces had turned into vicious animals with fangs, and that scared me. I knew their sins had turned them into this state, and the original face was just the outer layer. I stepped back, and the holy man stood from his chair. He opened his arm, and his cloak fell above my head. He said, 'For as long as you are under my clock, no one will ever harm you. You are safe.' And I felt calm. I felt secure, and I knew he was going to protect me. At the time, I didn't know I had dreamt Psalms 91. Jesus was calling for me.

I was born into a Muslim family; however, I was never ostracised from knowing other religions. In fact, I was put into a Christian school from a young age, so Jesus has been with me all my life; I was just too blind to see. Even as a Muslim, he waited and patiently gave me signs to give my heart to him. My dream was just one of his signs. I was lost and struggling to find the reason.

I was tired of living and constantly battling with my troubles. Most importantly, I was broken. But when I met Babi, everything changed, and when we talked about the contradictions in Islam, I began to read more, and the more I read, I realized I had been lied to and doing it all wrong. Jesus spoke to me when I began reading John. Suddenly, I felt a rush in my body. I heard his voice and felt his presence. Tears came rolling down my eyes, I began shaking, and I immediately knew my life had been changed. I had been given a new heart. I repented and sought forgiveness. I forgave everyone who had done me wrong and asked for healing power because I wanted to help everyone suffering - like I have been. I felt utter joy and as if everything had been wiped away.

Since then, my perspective has changed. I am utterly devoted to his words and relish in his presence. He talks to me and has become my heart, body, spirit, and soul.

I am here today to be baptized because- I love you, Jesus. Just like you asked me to stay under your cloak and stay protected, I now ask you to keep me there and never leave my side. I am dedicating my life to you.

JAMES 1:12

BLESSED ARE THOSE WHO PERSEVERE UNDER TRIAL, BECAUSE WHEN THEY HAVE STOOD THE TEST, THEY WILL RECEIVE THE CROWN OF LIFE THAT GOD HAS PROMISED TO THOSE WHO LOVE HIM. NIV